Love Leans over the Table

Rosie Jackson

For Annie —
warmest wishes

Rosie
September 2024 x

TWO
RIVERS
PRESS

By the same author

Fantasy: The Literature of Subversion (Methuen, 1981)
The Eye of the Buddha and Other Therapeutic Tales
    (Women's Press, 1991)
Frieda Lawrence (Harper Collins, 1994)
Mothers Who Leave (Harper Collins, 1994)
What the Ground Holds (Poetry Salzburg, 2014)
The Light Box (Cultured Llama, 2016)
The Glass Mother: A Memoir (Unthank, 2016)
Two Girls and a Beehive: Poems about Stanley Spencer and Hilda Carline
    (with Graham Burchell) (Two Rivers Press, 2020)
Aloneness is a Many-Headed Bird (with Dawn Gorman)
    (Hedgehog Press, 2020)
Light Makes it Easy (Indigo Dreams Publishing, 2021)

Also by Two Rivers Poets

David Attwooll, *The Sound Ladder* (2015)
Charles Baudelaire, *Paris Scenes* translated by Ian Brinton (2021)
William Bedford, *The Dancers of Colbek* (2020)
Kate Behrens, *Man with Bombe Alaska* (2016)
Kate Behrens, *Penumbra* (2019)
Kate Behrens, *Transitional Spaces* (2022)
Conor Carville, *English Martyrs* (2019)
David Cooke, *A Murmuration* (2015)
David Cooke, *Sicilian Elephants* (2021)
Tim Dooley, *Discoveries* (2022)
Jane Draycott, *Tideway* (re-issued 2022)
Jane Draycott & Lesley Saunders, *Christina the Astonishing* (re-issued 2022)
Claire Dyer, *Interference Effects* (2016)
Claire Dyer, *Yield* (2021)
John Froy, *Sandpaper & Seahorses* (2018)
James Harpur, *The Examined Life* (2021)
Maria Teresa Horta, *Point of Honour* translated by Lesley Saunders (2019)
Ian House, *Just a Moment* (2020)
Philippe Jaccottet, *In Winter Light* translated by Tim Dooley (2022)

Love Leans over the Table

Rosie Jackson is a widely published poet and creative writing tutor living in Teignmouth, Devon. She has a first-class BA Hons degree in English & Comparative Literature from the University of Warwick, a DPhil from York, and has taught at the Universities of East Anglia, West of England, Nottingham Trent, Skyros Writers' Centre, Cortijo Romero and many community settings. A Hawthornden Fellow in 2017 and nominated for the Pushcart Prize in 2021, Rosie has won numerous awards and has collaborated with other poets, artists, sculptors, musicians and film-makers. She has worked with the creative arts in health care, and her spiritual life has taken her to India and the United States.

www.rosiejackson.org.uk

Gill Learner, *Chill Factor* (2016)

Gill Learner, *Change* (2021)

Sue Leigh, *Chosen Hill* (2018)

Sue Leigh, *Her Orchards* (2021)

Becci Louise, *Octopus Medicine* (2017)

Mairi MacInnes, *Amazing Memories of Childhood, etc.* (2016)

Steven Matthews, *On Magnetism* (2017)

Steven Matthews, *Some Other Where* (2023)

Henri Michaux, *Storms under the Skin* translated by Jane Draycott (2017)

Kate Noakes, *Goldhawk Road* (2023)

René Noyau, *Earth on Fire and other Poems* translated by Gérard Noyau
    with Peter Pegnall (2021)

James Peake, *Reaction Time of Glass* (2019)

James Peake, *The Star in the Branches* (2022)

Peter Robinson & David Inshaw, *Bonjour Mr Inshaw* (2020)

Peter Robinson, *English Nettles* (re-issued 2022)

Peter Robinson, *Retrieved Attachments* (2023)

Lesley Saunders, *Nominy-Dominy* (2018)

Lesley Saunders, *This Thing of Blood & Love* (2022)

Jack Thacker, *Handling* (2018)

Robin Thomas, *The Weather on the Moon* (2022)

Susan Utting, *Half the Human Race* (2017)

Jean Watkins, *Precarious Lives* (2018)

First published in the UK in 2023 by Two Rivers Press
7 Denmark Road, Reading RG1 5PA.
www.tworiverspress.com

ISBN 978-1-915048-07-3

4 5 6 7 8 9

Two Rivers Press is represented in the UK by Inpress Ltd
and distributed by Ingram Publisher Services UK.

Cover painting: *Two Agapanthus* by Winifred Nicholson, 1980, oil on canvas,
51 cm x 41 cm. Private Collection. © Trustees of Winifred Nicholson
Cover and text design by Nadja Guggi and typeset in Janson and Parisine

Printed and bound in Great Britain by Severn, Gloucester

Acknowledgements

I am grateful to the editors of journals and online magazines in which some of these poems first appeared: *Acumen, Alchemy Spoon, Artemis, As Above So Below, Finished Creatures, Frogmore Papers, Glow, High Window, The North, Pennine Platform, Poetry and All that Jazz, Poetry Ireland Review, Raceme, Scintilla.* Several of the poems also appeared on 'Write Where We Are Now', an online poetry project edited by Carol Ann Duffy at www.mmu.ac.uk. And to the editors of anthologies *Phenomenal Women* (Grey Hen, 2021) and *Locked Down* (Poetry Space, 2021).

Some poems appeared in *Aloneness is a Many-Headed Bird* (with Dawn Gorman, Hedgehog Press, 2020).

'Imaginary Prisons' was written for B-Wing, an arts installation and poetry project funded by Arts Council England, at Shepton Mallet Prison, 2019.

'The Golden Bough' was commissioned for *Christmas Spirit* (Candlestick Press, 2019).

'Barbara Hepworth Considers the Visitors at Trewyn' was made into a poetry film by Gordon McKerrow, YouTube, 2018.

Thank you to the judges and organisers of poetry competitions in which some of the poems were placed or commended:

'After Reading Wendy Pratt's *When I Think of My Body as a Horse*', prize winner *Poetry News*, Poetry Society, Summer 2021.

'A Medic Learns to Darn in the Dissecting Room', 2nd prize *Frogmore Papers*, 2018.

'An Anchorite Laments the Destruction of her Cell', Highly Commended Winchester, 2018.

'Ancrene Wisse', 3rd prize *Acumen*, 2021.

'Don't Think These Doors Will Ever Close', Commended Hippocrates Open, 2021.

'George Fox Learns of the Great Fire', Long-listed Bridport, 2019.

'In Which I Ask Forgiveness of My Body', Commended Grey Hen, 2021.

'John Donne Arriving in Heaven', Joint 1st prize Bath Poetry Café, 2015.

'John Donne Dreams his Still-Born Son Lives', 3rd prize Kent and Sussex, 2022.

'One Little Roome, An Every Where', 1st prize Wells, 2018.

'The Artist's View of Surgery', Commended Hippocrates Open, 2019.

'The Boisterous Sobbings of Margery Kempe', Commended Poets and Players, 2022.

'The Day Meher Baba Died', Short-listed Bridport, 2022.

'The Woman Who Lives at the Back of the Quaker Meeting House', Commended Grey Hen, 2022.

'Where Bluebells Are Thickest', 1st prize Poetry Space, 2019.

I am deeply grateful to Moniza Alvi for her generous and inspired mentoring, also to Moniza, Jenny Lewis and Kim Moore for their endorsements. Thanks to Veronica Aaronson, Chrissy Banks, Ian Royce Chamberlain, Claire Dyer, Dawn Gorman, Nikki Kenna, Sue Proffitt, Wayne Smith, Tessa Strickland and Knucklebone poets for their support and close readings. And to Peter Robinson, Anne Nolan, all at Two Rivers Press, and to many poetry friends. Thanks also to the Trustees of the Winifred Nicholson estate for kind permission to reproduce on the front cover her 1980 painting *Two Agapanthus* and to Annie Freud for leading me to it.

Love me listened ech word
And begh him to me over bord
And bad me for to hente that hord
Of myn herte hele…

(Love listened to my every word
And leaned to me over the table
And bade me take hold of that treasure
Of my heart's healing…)

— 'Blow, Northerne Wind', 14th century

Contents

II. Better than Angels

III. Among Mortals

I. Hearken, O Daughter

Hildegard's Remedy

And when a man's mind is buried like coal under the earth,
tie round his head a cloth in which sit cooked grains of wheat.
And let the softened wheat carry to his disheartened mind
memory of warm bread, the comfort of a kitchen where love
holds the ladle, a field where poppies and mice exult in summer.
Then clouds will pass, darkness and delirium will be shot through
like thunder riddled by light. And when the cloth is unwound,
the man will smile for the first time in months. He will pluck a blade
of grass taller than his hands, put it to his lips and make it sing.

The Covenant

starts here, Pinderfields Hospital, my dad
flat on his thirty-something back for months,
a year, torso in plaster, legs inglorious in traction.
I'm standing near the bed in my smocked dress,
hand-knitted bolero. I've just learned to walk.
And Dad longs to take me in his arms, throw me
to the ceiling, stroll to Headingley, smell the soot
of Leeds, lean on a gate to smoke a Woodbine.

Of course he doesn't say no when two strangers
arrive out of the New Testament, gleaming with
faith, dripping with the River Jordan.
He'll swear to any promise, sign any bargain,
keep forever the thin white handkerchief
they lay on him, fold it into his leather Bible,
attend church every Sunday for the rest of his life
if God will send his tuberculosis packing.

So when I'm three, four, five, eight, ten years old,
my father and I go each week, hand in hand,
to High Anglican mass. We recite the creed by heart,
sight saints and spirits in the clouds of frankincense.
And from the way Dad gazes at that milky life-sized
body on the cross, I too know – of course I do –
it can step down any moment to humour us,
grant us anything.

In a Cold Place

Prayer got Dad through most things. Like that day
he was trapped in the freezer at work, shoulder
to shoulder with fatted calves and sugar-pink pigs
who dangled by their trotters, the hairs on their ears
hard as tufts of icy grass in winter.

Surely he gave thanks when some unlikely angel –
a bloodied workmate at the abattoir – came
to rescue him. Surely he dreamt, in that place
of implacable coldness, of his wife, two kids,
the half-life he'd always lived, as something

all at once precious, warm, full of such possibilities,
he promises, nay swears on his soul – if he's allowed
to return – he will find the courage to run
towards, tenderly manhandle.

The Ground We Stand On

My grandfathers were blackened by seams of coal.
Tibshelf, Sutton, Pleasley, Clay Cross, Glapwell,

were my family's scrag end of the woods, slagheaps
our mountains near the landlocked spine of the country.

The green bit on the map was Hardwick Hall,
where my mother knew Bess' family tree better than her own.

Mum left school at fourteen to work in a stocking factory where,
she said, her mother, Emma, had lost three fingers in a machine.

My father, by day a rat catcher and meat inspector, by night
a poet, recited Shakespeare at supper (we called it tea),

much to my mother's displeasure. She longed for a real bloke
who could mend cars, win the pools, have a backbone

that wouldn't cave in to illness as Dad's did. All the virtues
I loved him for – kind, generous, God-fearing, tender –

were too mild for my mother, who wanted a Rhett Butler –
and she put my father down till he lay, far too young, in the earth.

Torn between the two of them, I was caught between loving men
and despising them; the dilemma compounded when I drowned

in the second wave of feminism. It can take a long time
to find our life's work – to learn what real loving is.

Wayside

Walking for hours along disused railway
tracks with my book, my bag of apples,
striding over black oak sleepers, thinking
of trains that carried kids from our pit village
to Cleethorpes, Skegness – as if we too might
be changed into ruddy poster children
grinning against a backdrop of white-laced
waves with picnics, clean socks, buckets
and spades. And loving how tall they were,
the rosebay willow herbs that sprouted
down the edge of cinder tracks – wild, purple,
profligate. I didn't know their Latin name
then – *Chamaenerion angustifolium* –
but I loved how they took their chance,
how coal dust couldn't stop them,
how tangled seed-heads repopulated
fallow ground with such abandon,
how roots struck rhizomes into gravel.
In the south, I'm told, they attract
the rare Four-Spotted Furrow Bee –
Lassioglossum quadrinotatum –
but I never saw anything so golden.
Only ants, flies, nameless black things,
hungry, as we all are, for nectar.

Letter to Nietzsche

Dear Friedrich,

I learnt you by rote on the number 7 bus,
my satchel bulging with homework and atheism.
I'd quote from *The Anti-Christ, The Birth of Tragedy.*
And since you'd said, '*God is dead*' with such clout,
how could I not hold my dad in contempt as he bowed
to the crucifix with its coy loin cloth, not scorn Mum
as she fell to her knees each night beside the chamber pot?
I worshipped every secular giant because I craved
delivery from slavery in the Metal Box factory,
streets with the country's highest murder rate.

Yet today, when I saw you on Facebook,
that posthumous portrait by Edvard Munch –
a man on a bridge, same composition
as *The Scream*, same lurid agony of a sky –
I learned for the first time how very ill
you were: migraines, despair, dementia,
a slow death from syphilis. And I thought
how easy it is for darkness to turn us
into goliaths, how hard to say yes
to being toppled by tiny pebbles of love.

What a long time it can take to wake up.
I missed fifty years of cherry blossom.
Mocking their faith broke my parents' hearts.
But sometimes, Friedrich, in an empty church,
I'll walk to the altar, kneel by the rail.
When I open my eyes to angels I haven't
noticed before, I post them on line with
their *oud*, *ney*, lyre. I love how their wan faces
seem to care, yet not care. I love how
they never apologise.

His Heart Like Wax

When I think of my father I think of a man
incompetent in the ways of the world, unable

to put up shelves, mend cars, handle solicitors,
know what to do to stop bad things happening.

He lives inside a kind of holy loneliness, reads
the Psalms like a love letter, feels the world

weigh heavy in his arms. He knows what it is
to long for peace, to inhabit days that work him

looser and looser, his body barely attached
to his chair, his wife, his unmanageable kids,

all those slaughtered animals he works with.
And so I think of love like this, of God like this,

infinitely kind, well-meaning, full of goodness,
but always on the back foot, not quite managing.

The Day Meher Baba Died

I'm 17. My bedroom in our council house
has two divans draped with black and white throws.
So much is black and white. There's life and
there's death. There's others and there's me.
I'm hungry. I skip breakfast. I've lost so much
weight I've been struck off the hockey team.
At 7.45am I take the number 7 bus. I sit
on school radiators to keep warm, read
Francois Mauriac's *Le Noeud de Vipères*
for A-level. The skies have not gone dark,
though floods in Mecca have made the Kaaba
unreachable. I have no idea what the word
'Kaaba' means. I have never heard of Allah.
I'm a year away from messing up my life.
In 3 years my father will die. In 43 years my mother
will die. In 10 years I will know this date better
than my own birthday. I will be in love with a man
who today is surrounded by ice and flowers.
Across India phones are ringing. People are rushing
for trains and flights. Trucks of ice are driving
up the hill that will one day be my sanctuary.
I skip lunch. Hour by hour I grow lighter.
I am more dead than alive. In the fierce
Maharashtrian sunset, crowds gather. He
is more alive than dead. A portable gramophone
plays 'Begin the Beguine' – *To live it again
is past all endeavour...* On the bus home, I memorise
quotes from Mauriac. I wear a navy beret.
It's February tomorrow. I'm waiting to hear
which university has offered me a place. I'm
predicted 3 As. I'm as ignorant as Formica.
It's 1969. I have a decade of emptiness ahead
of me. 10 more years of not knowing anything.
Then a lifetime letting in what's happened today.

The Night I Grew Old

There was no bed. Just a tangle of improvised sheets
where we lay, young, half-conscious. But I knew
straight away – don't ask me how, an angel tore
aside the curtain – a new life had arrived inside me,
its invisible heft so huge, like a meteor trailing light,
I thought all Nottingham must be woken by it.
But no. The city slept. The father slept, as men often do,
afterwards. And all that never-to-be-the-same-again
night, as I lay in shock on our friends' floor, I worried
what soul would choose such unpropitious circumstance
to swim into this world, knew without being told
this child would demand of me the impossible, that I
was sliding towards a test I could not pass. By the time
dawn bleached that shabby room, the child I was
had already started to turn into that woman on the wall –
The Lady of Shalott – her pre-Raphaelite hair trailing
into a boat which would carry her downstream,
her luscious mouth a terror of uprootedness.

Don't Think These Doors Will Ever Close

after 'Maternity', by Dorothea Tanning 1946–7

You've forgotten what a pillow is for,
what easels and gardens are for. Wakefulness
licks your feet, your body is frayed at the edge.
Loss of sleep has slipped you onto sand
the yellow of wedding rings, your heart
pounding with the weight of a child, ears open

to every new-born in the world, eyes open
to melancholy, nighthawk and grackle. For
door after door is now ajar inside your heart,
your new familiar a wakefulness
that measures time in milk spilt onto sand,
your nights spent staring over the edge

of the world as if it were flat again, an edge
as fragile as paper. You didn't expect to be wedged open
like this, to stand vigilant on desert sand
under storm clouds – *nimbus, mammatus* – alert for
every child that crawls towards your wakefulness.
Every infant that barks neglect. You're shocked by your heart

and its unspeakable love, love that stretches a heart
beyond its limits, just as your skin tore at the edge
when a child pushed through. Yet wakefulness
feels part of that dream in which you were split open,
excavated, months of heaviness removed, before
you met this unlikely version of yourself on sand

quick in its undoing. This is sand

that will make you anonymous, pull your heart
into a ghost of itself, dull your appetite for
the masculine lure of the city. You're beyond the edge
of that high-rise world now, out in the open,
stranded in a ragged frame of wakefulness

where only mothers stand – the kind of wakefulness
that has you dressing hurriedly on the sand,
a dark sky watching, doors and walls left open.
Expect no more ease of solitude within your heart,
no more privacy. Expect bread cut with a jagged edge.
For this is what birth delivers: breasts leaking for

pity of the world, heart prised open,
long sands of wakefulness, a woman on the edge.
A child who knows what your body is for.

After Reading Wendy Pratt's
When I Think of My Body as a Horse

I did that thing you talk about – lay my naked baby
on my naked body, his ear pressed like a stethoscope
against my chest so he would hear my heart lub-dubbing
in his deep-sleeping brain.

We lived over a hairdresser's, my son's new-born smell
polluted by shampoo and lacquer, and from 9 to 5
piped music drifted through their ceiling, our floor,
Rod Stewart's *Maggie May*, or *Chirpy Chirpy Cheep Cheep*.

There were still phones then in red boxes on street corners,
and when I suffered from post-natal kleptomania,
there were no CCTV cameras in our old-fashioned pharmacy
to catch me as I purloined life-sized lemons made of soap,

each with its own rope for hanging. In no time
my yellow harvest turned our windowless bathroom
into a Mediterranean courtyard, lit up for a fiesta
with sweet-smelling citrus trees. And I remember

vowing to him, this few-days-out-of-my-body baby –
already too big to believe he had ever squeezed in there –
swearing, as we lay in our skin-to-skin mantle, that no one,
nothing, would ever come between us.

We were mammals, after all, we belonged in the same
sett of mud and blood and leaves. Even the din of
rumbling traffic or drills (we were on a main arterial road)
only drove us closer into our warm milky huddle.

But when the bough breaks, the cradle will fall.
I lost him, far too young, in a custody battle. And though
I know this isn't the same as death – he's a grown man now,
with a child of his own – whenever I hear of a mother's loss,

a riptide of grief maroons me once more in those nights
when I'd walk to red boxes to talk with him before he went
to bed. Someone was always laughing in the background.
Strangers would tap at the glass. I never had enough coins.

Coming to Terms With

trauma is a breach
                    in time's experience of the mind

    I mean the experience

of time is a trauma   no I mean trauma is a breach

  in the mind   I mean   experience is a trauma

      to a mind in breach   I mean the mind   is

a trauma   I mean in the mind's experience   time

is a breach no   in the   experience of   trauma

        the mind is not in time the mind   is a breach

in time   in the time of trauma   the mind is not   no

                I mean trauma is a breach in   experience

    I mean the mind   is an experience

  I mean trauma   is

an experience I mean   experience in time is

    a breach   of trauma I mean

    trauma is a breach in the mind's   experience of time

My Father Tries to Make Amends

All I have left of him is his Bible, in Pitman's shorthand,
its cover black, vanilla-coloured pages leafed with gold.

He was a quiet man – not given to rapture or controversy.
The sound of him riddling the ashes woke me in winter

and how proud he was of me in my school uniform,
or walking me to church twice each Sunday.

Be good sweet maid and let who will be clever,
urged his copperplate in my autograph book,

and at my shot-gun wedding, he sobbed like a widow.
No one could deliver him then from his black dog.

The next year he opted out of being a father
altogether. Unless you count the help he likes to offer

from the afterlife – when I confess that cleverness
didn't work, and he admits that goodness

didn't do much either. We sit with his heavy Bible
in front of us, his light hand lifting the pages as it did

when I was a child. He reminds me of the 'c'
that means *with*, 'v's that soar like kites' wings,

the simplicity of those mysteries veiled in hieroglyphs –
words like *mercy, tabernacle* – he still loves to decipher.

And I hear the familiar sound of his whisper – *hyssop, lilies,
hearken O daughter, I am poured out like water, my heart is like wax.*

Revisiting *The Garden of Earthly Delights* at the Prado

I lived here once, trapped in this mussel shell, lodged
against mucus. Those are my skinny ankles trying to hook
better dreams. And here's my mother, half horse, half hollow
egg. How she disliked the neighbours, medieval riff-raff,
their nakedness a kind of warfare, vaginal pink palaces,
bodies half-regressed to swine and porcupine.

Hell in the right-hand panel, Eden in the left, but not heaven –
gender still spills everywhere. God standing in the first field,
steering Eve by the wrist to give her to Adam, this man sprawled
on the ground with magpies and rabbits. Purple grapes twine
round the nearest tree. Eve's hair weighs more than she does.

I used to love Bosch. I put him on the cover of my first book.
But now, I go in search of El Greco's lengthened bodies straining –
like Christ in that other garden – between this world and the next.

Talking with My Imaginary Sister

When I wake at dawn and the truth
of the world hits again, I find myself
longing for a sister who will listen
with me to wood pigeons by the open skylight,
who knows me through and through, recalls
those marriages where she was my maid of honour,
nights of pouring whisky over our
broken hearts.
             I mean a real flesh-and-blood sister,
the same flawed DNA, a sister yellow
as a tree peony, who calls me a phoenix,
remains curious, carries the trowel
to the side of the lake when we bury
our mother's ashes, enjoys me telling her
about rhododendron buds sprouting pink
on that spot each April after she's moved
to New York.
          A sister who doesn't mind
when I forget the time difference,
call too early on Good Friday, tell her
this lockdown is like having my feet
tied together, my brain clamped
in one of those old-fashioned hairdryers
that rose towards the ceiling like Klaus Kinski's
helmet in Herzog's *Wrath of God*.
And does she think this plague could be
some kind of reckoning?
             A sister who knows
how to step through stations of the cross,
looks forward to the third day, reminds me
of races we ran at school, three-legged,
our ankles tied together with scarves, how
the restriction made us roll over with laughter,
how – in her version of events – we always won.

Like Jean Shrimpton

I don't remember her name, but can still see the bike:
a red Triumph Bonneville. I never knew a girl could
wear leathers, have something so noisy between her legs.
When she walked into a bar, men fell silent. She looked
like Jean Shrimpton. I was shocked when she approached me.
Men's wishes were stamped on me like fingerprints. The ink
was still wet from my husband's fumbling. When my son came
for holidays, she was the one who took him hunting for crabs
and lobsters. She wasn't butch, she just knew what to do.
I don't remember why we split up, I must have let her down
somehow. I got a moped I could barely manage: Honda 50.
I didn't know how to twist the throttle. Perhaps that was it.
She was so beautiful. She tasted so different from men.
In another generation, we'd be together. I'd ride pillion.

Blue

I'm at the hairdresser's, sieving through scandal
in gossipy mags, when I learn Joni Mitchell has a child,

a daughter she left behind decades ago. And I'm back
in that first Christmas, when I discovered her album *Blue*.

It was mid-winter cold, a slate quarry in North Wales,
my cabin musty with Calor gas and loneliness.

I chose the sleeve for its ultramarine, relished her icy voice,
forensic and boundless in its longing – *looking for something,*

what can it be? – played the track again and again, amazed
someone else knew the same unravelling, *that undoes*

all the joy that could be. But it's only now – *Hello! OK!* –
the penny finally drops. Now I understand the song

'Little Green'. Now my loss sits in the next chair
like a small child looking from all angles at the mirror.

And Would It Have Been Better

It is hard to see your son fall, to ask if
it would have been better not to give him a life

so scratched and badly started. Better to have
sent him back before his cells rooted too deeply,

back to that pre-formed unsuffering place of stars
and nebulae where souls float like unnamed planets

and he could wait for a happier night sky. Then
he'd have landed differently, found solid ground,

a world of trust and beech trees. But he came to me –
that was his choice. I kept him – that was mine,

a mix of grace and cowardice. So I watch him fall,
suffer the same helplessness I felt when his soft skull

squeezed through me, shocked again by the pain
a woman is expected to bear without dying.

Grief: A User's Guide

Follow the instructions carefully. Do not use your grief
for purposes other than the one for which it is intended.
Extreme caution must be taken.

Lift your grief, do not drag. If you meet any resistance,
cut into pieces. Gently shake if necessary.
Ensure the grief is vented away from you.

Your grief is fitted with a quick release mechanism.
Never force your grief and especially do not
apply force to the Open/Close switch.

Excess grief should be safely and gently released
through the hole in the top.
Do not allow flames to speed up the sides.

Do not let children near your grief.
In the unlikely event of grief reaching higher levels
than normal, the safety device will operate.

Check to ensure there are no additional splits, tears or cracks.
Do not stand in water. Avoid adding salt to your grief,
as this may result in pitting. If necessary, tighten.

You might try vinegar, lemon juice, or apple peeling.
Avoid excessive pressure. Avoid scourers.
Never use bleach to clean your grief.

If you need help, please contact us. Your grief
is guaranteed to last for twelve months
under normal use. Bodies cannot be repaired.

Stroke

i.m. Gay Clifford 1943–1998

She'd hold seminars in her cottage, the kitchen full
of Italian ceramics, fridge empty except for a jar of capers.
She'd wear white silk for meetings – a suit good enough
to die in – the gold vein in her black onyx ring a streak
of lightning as she spoke. In vacations she'd lend me
her office, send letters from Tuscany, typed in red.
She described this world as a palimpsest, layer upon layer
of meaning waiting to be peeled away. I still have her book,
that quote from Donne about Truth residing on a tall hill,
cragged and steep, our souls trudging round to reach the top.

A short-lived marriage. Hidden illnesses. Then, one Christmas
Eve, a massive stroke. And hair that used to stream back
like the black mane of a ship's figurehead was pinned ingloriously
with Kirby grips. Her body rolled out of shape. Words vanished
as she turned the page. Even the photo of her beloved
E. P. Thompson, leaning life-sized against the wall, could not
reanimate her brilliance. Once, desperate to retrieve her
from her living death, I blurted out, *Is there some meaning
for our illnesses*? And for the fiercest moment, she flashed back
to this world, her eyes angry stars. That's years ago now.

She's long gone. But I'll never forget all she taught me,
her love of allegory, the pleasure and power of *speaking other.*
Her favourite tale, for example, *The Green Knight*, who invites
Gawain to strike at his giant's neck with an axe, then strolls
away with his severed head under his arm – I often think
that was her, wiping out her torment in one fell swoop.
I imagine her now in the garden of a medieval romance,
all brightness restored, urging me on as she did when I left
my own teaching post and fled to India. *Yes*, she smiles,
yes, there are less brutal ways to make the head bow to the neglected heart.

How Can We Bear It?

When we are ready, people are sent to help us surrender
to the un-knowing. I was sent George Barker,

T.S. Eliot's protégé, who introduced me to a poet's invisible
oceans and rills. I'd invited him to read to a group

of undergraduates, but only a handful turned up.
What did they care about an ageing, priapic poet,

who'd fathered fifteen children? It wasn't for them he came,
singing of Blake and Yeats. It was to awaken me,

to make me see through his eyes the concrete wasteland
of a modern campus: windowless corridors, left-brain

questions on the wall. As soon as he came into my office,
he gestured around, looked me in the eye, asked,

'*How can you bear it?*' That seed of a question levered me
out of my prestigious job, snaked me down the ladder

leading to a stout pension, changed me from a shoulder-padded
academic stalking the city into a poet in a short red dress,

heading west in search of her tribe. Folly, I see that now,
from a worldly point of view, to fall under the spell of words,

to live near the breadline. But I learned to love margins,
flotsam, weeds, wilds, fells. I learned to hear things in shells.

Let's Call it Light

I don't remember which novel I had on the go,
what my rituals were for sleeping, but I do recall
it was November, I was alone in the house, the bedroom
had chocolate walls, a Chagall print over the brass bed.
I'd pulled the curtains my mother made against the distant
street light, put out my lamp, was probably thinking about
the video of India I'd seen that evening, when it arrived.
Is *light* even the right word for what happened?

Is sun the right word, moon, stars, glory of a million
galaxies? Let's call it light, to be approximate, let's watch it
expand, as I watched, from a pinprick of gold, an unexpected
floater to a roomful, houseful, dissolver of walls, city of light.
Let's call it that, this yellow epiphany that grew and grew,
swallowed me into it, erased me, though this wasn't loss,
it was being caught inside an infinite benevolence –
the words are missing by miles. It was alpha and omega,

it was a joyful shining holiness, an eternal gob-smacking light
that wrapped me in something I'd never known, never imagined,
love, God, bliss, happiness, whatever the words are for that world
of light (let's call it that), a radiance I thought the preserve of those
who've died. And it was a kind of death, the way giving birth
is a kind of death, the way it leaves you no choice but
to surrender, and I didn't exist anymore as me, though
even this non-existent me had light inside it.

And when, eventually, the light left, though of course it never
leaves, when eventually the light, God, this thing that had come
and never quite leaves left, there I was, 3am, in the same shaking,
shocked, wondering-what-tornado-had-passed-through-me state
as when my son was born, knowing the same sense of unknowing,
undoing, of having had pass through me the greatest mystery
there is, and all my life I would have the same bewilderment
I knew that night of not being able to put any of this into words.

II. Better than Angels

Tilting

after Marie Howe's 'Annunciation'

I want to tilt in that direction
as to the mirror where light first swam.
Even if I can't find it again
I want to tilt in that direction –
specifically myself yet no one –
to bear the love the shining is from.
Oh, let me tilt in that direction
as to the mirror where light first swam.

St Bede: From Winter to Winter

Look at me, half here, half not, caught
in this blue land between dust and light.
I fly into the dining hall where you sit
at supper, your illusion of flames in the grate.
I move on threads of air, follow the signs
of elsewhere rising. I brush the arms
of implausible beings, angels moving
slowly between snow and shadow.
No longer married to this world of bitter
oracles, I live on the very edge of speech,
retrieve words like *pilgrim*, *naked*, *celestial*.
Listen: if you would hear the gods breathe,
you must be stranded from yourself.
Even my passport says *sparrow*.

Rabia and the Thief

I imagine her here, in some quantum future,
her summers in hedgerows, winters in a corrugated shed
where she plays cards with God, who cheats, of course,

or plaits her hair, uncombed for centuries. She asks him
for a love that is out of this world and he replies
her soul is too old for trinkets. She does not lament

the garden of Eden, that sweet homeland between
the Tigris and Euphrates, once heavy with angels.
But prays for the whole earth to wake from pain,

to forgo its journeys to the black box of the Kaaba,
the crosses and synagogues, *asanas* of yoga,
all that greed for the milk and honey of heaven.

Nor does she grieve at the loss of her beauty,
but welcomes the truth of what she will become,
lets herself be scoured by that longing for union

when she will take between her hands the much-loved
face on which the seven worlds are written, marry
that silence whose love leaves all words behind.

I think of her most when it's hot at night and I open
the window, remember the thief who climbed
over the sill into her sparse bedroom. Would I do

what she did? Recognise the smell of ocean,
know the man as another creature out of water,
hair braided with kelp and badderlocks?

And, before he can snatch my blanket, fold
every piece of bedding, each last cotton sheet,
hand them to him like a dowry?

When I Wonder What It Was Like to Be an Anchorite

the nearest I can get is that day I locked myself
in the house, in one room, huddled in darkness.
It was January cold, I wore gloves and a beanie hat,
lay hunched on a makeshift mattress in what would
one day be the lounge. I was newly moved into
a ruin of a place, all stone and draughts. For days
I'd made builders' tea, talked builders' talk, and now
they were fixing the roof, but I was weary of the world,
craved peace and silence. I couldn't put on the light,
in case they saw, or listen to the radio, in case they heard,
or have a fire, for smoke would travel to them up
the chimney. All day I lay in darkness while shouts
and sounds of hammering came from another world,
as an anchorite would listen to men mending
the church roof. It felt miraculous, like being
at the bottom of the sea. In their lunch break,
suspecting I was there, for my car was in the drive,
they came close to the window, made smutty jokes,
wondered where I peed, mocked single women
who don't, after all, have much of a handle
on the world. And perhaps an anchorite knew
the same relief I felt that day, when the sweetness
of dusk finally fell, the hammering stopped,
the men packed up their tongues and clatter
and darkness was once again mine, all mine.
I could breathe, pray, praise and curse out loud
without anyone, except God perhaps, listening.

The Anchorite's Mother

feels sick, as nauseous as those early weeks
when this daughter was entombed inside her,
her body off-balance like a ship at sea.

Her daughter claims this world is glass, brittle
and short-lived compared to the other kingdom,
but these walls are mighty thick to transform into light,

the squint barely large enough to pass a chamber pot.
She wants to stuff the cell with bluebells, jay feathers,
to remind her child of sky in summer.

What upside-down creator would take such trouble
to make life, if He wanted it cast away? She thinks
of a sprig of willow trampled, heel by heel,

into the ground. That farewell smile, timid, hopeful,
is the same her other daughter wore when she married,
before the back of her husband's hand wiped it away.

Why does no one talk of God's back of hand?
Is not the Bible full of women's bruises? But now
the last stones and handfuls of mud are wedged

into place. The eye closes. The angelus sounds.
God has chastened, made chaste, blinded her daughter.
A mother can do nothing but bring food, water.

See her stumble home, lament as if it were a wake.
How fiercely she feeds the fire, breaks the neck
of a chicken, stays up all night to bake.

One Little Roome, An Every Where

The damp walls are closer than the stretch of her arm.
There's a stench of sea, and she floats alongside miracles
of lobsters, crabs, creyvish, who swim and crawl

in the ignorance of praise, not yet upright
on the dry land of arrogance and doubt.
Her cell clings like a barnacle to the church,

where men in albs and chasubles shout of hell,
while she does the real work, heeds the small
voice of God in the darkness. This is the space

behind the boulder which will be rolled
away, the thick blackness in which trees take root,
where all that is to come seeds and quickens.

Love is not the right word. Love is too cushiony
for a woman who sleeps on stone, kneels on stone,
prays with the steadfastness of granite.

It's like staying awake inside sleep, this being
allowed inside the mind of God, a great cave
of nothingness that knows everything,

just she and He together, as intense as if summer
has been preserved in honey and she can hold it
on her tongue whenever she needs to taste some sweetness.

If she grows curious about what it is to be married,
she only has to touch herself, and a sea anemone
unfurls. Opens until she knows she is nothing but water.

But where a wife would cup her husband's face
between her hands, feel his bearded jaw hard
against her palm, she has no need to hold the face of God.

His eyes are on her constantly, *washed with milk
and fitly set.* His *head is filled with dew.* And there is
no word for the tenderness between them

as they drop anchor for those crowded ships of fools
who have forgotten why their souls embarked
on this brief crossing of a life at all.

The Recluse Tells of her Love

Here I am untrusset[1] of all worldly woes.
Here I am undeadlich[2]. I am the spus[3] of the Lord.
He is my leofmon[4]. I untouch[5] all else save him.
Unhope[6] have I none. The waters cannot
acwenchen[7] my love, the floods cannot drown it.
In this death cell I am unburiet[8]. All that is unhal[9]
is locked out. Godd wat[10], but life is a schadewe[11]
that ne geine[12] o me nawt. What need have I
of huni[13]? I have ure lauerd seolf[14], yea the very lord,
Godd hisself is with me, his brethe swote,
smellinge of lavender and mire[15]. We kep
wecchen together, we sleppe nat, we dreme nat,
we think on his passion unendeliche.
His passion, that brings reowfulnesse[16]
and draws my sawle[17] to him, ever closer, ever
mere tenderlich. Forgit the little cote[18]
with the fire and bairns, forget the imperfect make[19].

1   untrusset   released, unbound
2   undeadlich   eternally alive
3   spus   wife
4   leofmon   sweetheart, lover, beloved
5   untouch   keep away from
6   unhope   despair
7   acwenchen   quench
8   unburiet   unburied
9   unhal   unholy
10   wat   knows
11   schadewe   shadow
12   geine   gain
13   huni   honey
14   ure lauerd seolf   our lord himself
15   mire   myrrh
16   reowfulnesse   sorrow
17   sawle   soul
18   cote   house
19   make   mate

This is my spus, this perfect one, this is my gleade[20],
and never was wumman more in parais[21]
than here in this little roome. The worlde,
I say again, ne geine o me nawt. But I streche
my luve to Iesu Crist, he I would wunne[22],
him I rin[23] wi as muche luve as I have sum mon rin.
Think me nat as one of your undeor[24] wummen.
Think me rather a wumman of widewehad[25],
unmeteliche[26] leof[27] of Godd hisself,
unmeteliche gleade, unmeteliche i-gracet[28].
Wat Crist, this is nat wacnesse, this gastelich[29] life,
this is parais and here I am unendliche gleade,
unendliche hal[30], with the meast[31] make, Godd seolf,
leof Godd, myn leofman, myn make.

20   gleade   joy, joyful
21   parais   paradise
22   wunne   win
23   rin   run to
24   undeor   cheap
25   widewehad   widowhood
26   unmeteliche   immeasurably
27   leof   beloved, love
28   i-gracet   blessed
29   gastelich   ghostly
30   hal   holy
31   meast   most/best

Ancrene Wisse

Not the first day. She's too full of the novelty
of dying. Nor the second, when pilgrims bring her
fresh-baked bread, the smell of yeast and wonder.

For weeks the pomp of her burial, the surprise
of her courage, uplift her. But as stone-rise follows
stone-rise, her feet grow restless. Regret feasts on her.

Sins start to stack like dirty pewter. She dreams
too much of the light of *before*, before this whale
of a god swallowed her whole, married her

to an endless dark *after*. Nor does she glimpse heaven
when she prays, but celandine, coastline, clearings
in a wood. She longs for hawks, the blue of midsummer.

As for *The Ancrene Wisse*, its writer free as a ferret, she
can't reach its brotherly pieties. No need for warnings
about spiritual pride, she's already failed her enclosure,

willing to recant every vow if she might walk the length
of a cloister. As for denying her Lord, the cock crows
for her. Are her first loves now not doors and windows?

A Kind of Divorce

No. We're not ashamed of sex, do not hate
each other, have not run out of money,
are not averse to children, don't compete
for God, are not Adam and Eve walking
backwards to undo the fall, not timid
in the world, not taken over by pride,
nor afraid to watch our loss of beauty.

We chose the hallowed route of separate cells,
dank walls, because we want to give ourselves
to ourselves the way we drop into death,
to hold the door open for each other
because our love gives us something we want
more of, because we want the first version
of ourselves like rain falls into water.

There Will Be No Epitaph

First I died to my feet. Then I died to my pride.
I died to sweat. I died to sleep.
I died to warm bread and bee orchids.
I died to apples pulping in my mouth.
I died to honeysuckle. I died to sun from the south.
I died to nettles and long grass.
I died to minnows swimming in the beck.
I died to snow. I died to rain on my back.
I died to gossip. I died to plainsong.
I died to trumpets and tambourines.
I died to skin. I died to my babies unborn.
I died to a mackerel sky. I died to colour.
Oh, I died to colour, as if He has no patience
with turquoise and madder.

The Long Text (Julian of Norwich)

They say she kept bees, that men bartered meat
for prayers and honey. They say she had a cat.
They say Christ came to her bed once, as intimate

and certain as death. And if she chose a cell, it was
to anchor his tenderness. If she took up knitting,
it was to go time after time into the same stitch,

to revisit that night like a widow reliving her wedding,
memory augmenting what could not bear to be lost.
They say she revered the sky because at his end

it splintered and grew dark. The first time she put
her *shewings* into words, it was a few sheets of vellum.
Twenty years on, she needed sacks of oak apples for ink.

They say she made *one-ing* into a verb, that hers
was the first book by a woman in English,
though she is known by the name of a man.

Many things get lost in churches. What is the word *God*,
after all, but an alias for the love that drew crowds
to the space in her cell we'd call a window, those sailors

trudging from docks to beg protection from waves
and pestilence. Then she'd tell them falling and rising
are the same when seen from the seeing of love,

that *'if there is on this earth a lover of God who is always kept safe,'*
she knew *'nothing of it.'* But yes, she would entreat blessings
on their sweethearts and babies. Her own child, they say,

was taken by the plague. Possibly her husband too.
We all have our ways of coping with grief. They say
her cell was pungent with mugwort, sage, lavender.

The Boisterous Sobbings
of Margery Kempe

And if she cries it's because her blood is thin,
the marrow sucked from her bones by fourteen children.
If she doesn't sleep, it's because God circles
her quarried pelvis like a buzzard, folds her over
like a prayer, pours her to the ground as if she's made
of water. If she falls out of herself, into herself,
repeats herself like a canticle, *Christus amor meus est*,
it's because the light of the world sits on her bed,
lets her know who she was before she splintered
into pieces. If mud spatters her skirt, if her head
is blue from banging on the ground, it's because
she knows the weight of love, the weight of a man hanging,
his body pulling down the sky, the world's suffering
pressing on his scalp like an inverted pyramid. If she rolls
in church aisles for priests to stumble over, it's because
their tongues are yellow with butter and cannot deliver
silence. If she grieves before bishops at Ely Cathedral,
it's because she's heard a girl in France has been set alight
for hearing sacred voices. If she accrues wealth in her mill
and brewery, it's to buy chastity from her husband,
servants for her children, travel to Spain, Jerusalem,
Rome. If she grieves over a splinter of wood from Calvary,
it's because this is a tree that has touched a man
with holes in his hands. And if she sobs before
Julian of Norwich, it's because she feels herself believed
at last by a woman who knows God is not a noun
but a verb: the very act of causing, birthing, doing,
dying, loving, moving, falling, rising. Everything.

An Anchorite Laments the Destruction of Her Cell in Henry VIII's Dissolution of the Monasteries, 1537

I laid down my life, so He could make wine out of me,
jug after jug. I wanted to be trodden by His feet.

But the Lord God has taken a battering ram to the heavens.
He has broken the night into pieces & days are too bright,

stars too sharp, prayers too feeble to be heard over such
great distances. Is this what it is to be scorched by the fires

of Love? Has devotion become so alien in this world,
it must be dismantled, stone by stone? I pick over the ruins

as if there's been an earthquake – a solitary, a woman who rattles
like a tinker with her pans, yet nothing to sell or mend. Oh, return me

to the discipline of the squint, the blind comfort of darkness.
Give me back the cover of His wings, my white apron of chastity.

I wasn't meant to be resurrected. My vow was unto death. This is how
Lazarus must have felt – nervous of each open space, raped by sunlight.

John Donne Dreams His Still-Born Son Lives

You arrive in a season of mallow and love-in-a-mist,
swim between worlds like a swordfish, eat little,
whittle wood into birds.

Like all children, you break things – teeth, bones,
your mother's heart. You like swimming in icy water,
retrieving almost-dead things under stones.

You talk to angels, know the exact hierarchy of cherubim
and seraphim, the pecking order from St. Michael down.
At night, I fancy your footsteps sound on bare boards

where you tread back and forth, reciting my poems.
I am a little world made cunningly Of Elements, and
an Angelike spright... You're my twelfth and last child –

I hesitate to say my favourite – but it's your face,
grown into manhood, riddled with sorrow, that I see
praying in the garden of Gethsemane. I like to think

you'll intercede for me. When I hear your voice, I hear
my own warm vowels, the same firm passion, faithful
consonants. It's strange how things are handed down,

like seeing yourself poured out again in a pitcher
of next year's water. But you move quickly, while I
stumble after you, not yet one of the immortals.

Many times in dreams I lose sight of you. You have my
slightly hooked nose, slender frame, long-fingered hands.
You'd make a good thief. As you did when you stole

your mother from me, your tiny face so unguarded,
raw, forlorn, she had no choice but to come with you.
If I could but love our *three-person'd God* with one shred

of the hunger I have for you and your mother.
See how I fall to my knees each morning, yellow with prayer
as the ivory gates close behind you once more.

Batter My Heart

Here's John Donne, wrestling with angels all night,
words that seem to have insufficient fire.
He twists and turns their heat into a knot,
fights to know the white taste of surrender.

And here, two centuries later, a man
who commits these same hard-won lines to heart.
He too paces the room, stays up till dawn
reciting Donne's fourteenth Holy Sonnet.

He repeats the poem over and over,
flooded with the same longing and hunger
for God to come and hammer at the door
of his narrow little room in Pune.

And because he learned it, I learn it too.
Batter my heart, I pray. *Take me to you.*

John Donne Arriving in Heaven

He knew it would be a melting, looking back
at the world as a place of icicles and clouds,
lilies of passion unmooring their tangled roots.

Knew that with the rungs of prayer and reason
knocked away, the subtle knot undone,
he would step into this delicate permanence,

the light cleansing, as protracted evening sun
perfects a field of harvest corn.
Expected such radiance that finds no flaws

in all that's happened, no severity,
only the mercy of a paradise always autumn,
its joy possessed, ripe, perfect, complete.

But this is less the arrival he foresaw
than an undoing of distances, a shedding
of himself to become who he already was,

not gaining union but losing the illusion
he was separate, was ever other than this one:
the hand that set all things in motion,

spread this equal light, made on a whim
the stars, the schoolboys, the unruly sun.
All love a dream of this. And now, as he takes on

the bliss, the infinite bliss his little deaths
on earth struggled to reach, he finds his words
at last translated to their proper tongue.

George Fox Learns of the Great Fire

1 September 1666
His first hours out of prison are always a wonder, the night folding back on itself like a blanket. Sometimes he thinks he knows the country by its prisons, their varieties of darkness – Nottingham, Derby, London, Leicester, Lancaster. And now Scarborough gaol left behind.

2 September
His footsteps sounding on the open road are such a joy to him. After so long inside, his walk is heavy, halting, determined. A white mist hovers over the North Sea. He thinks of God as this low-lying cloud, not quite touching us. He likes rain. He likes all weathers.

3 September
The morning sky is a visceral red as if something in the distance, a great cathedral say, has gone up in flames. Not that he would lament if all the churches of the land went up in flames. Such pieties of religion. As if God wanted anywhere but the simple chamber of the heart.

4 September
He loves the silence of walking alone. Ten years now since he came out from his time in Launceston prison and met Cromwell. And when he told him, 'God dwells not in temples made with hands', Cromwell agreed, wanted to meet again and sit with him in that quiet mystery.

5 September
He will doff his hat to no-one. He does not believe in outward forms. He thinks of this world as a place waiting to turn into itself, to become its own promise, wants to strip people back to their light.

6 September
News of the Great Fire in London reaches him in Yorkshire. He stands in the rain, prays for the hundreds of souls evicted from their bodies. He walks harder, prays harder. He stamps into the ground his rage that the poor are made to nest like rats, their walls burning like tinder.

7 September
He cannot stop thinking of them. Children of immigrants charred as they lay dreaming of sea under thatch and wattle.

8 September
He prays for the mothers holding their dead. He prays for the mothers who can't find their dead. He thinks of the clergy, patting the backs of mourners. The very same priests who deny women have souls.

9 September
Over a week of freedom already. His body is stronger now. He walks. He breaks bread. He talks to the skies. He prays for penance for Thomas Farynor, the man whose flame is said to have sparked the fire that set a city alight. How many dead? Who has an abacus large enough?

10 September–31 October
He walks. He walks and walks. Eight, twelve, eighteen, twenty-eight miles a day. He's like a dog herding his followers. Monthly meetings. Healings. Faith immovable as rock. Testimonies. Silent witness. Climbing the tall ladders of prayer.

5 November
The official numbers of the dead in London's Great Fire reach him. Six. Yes, sir, you heard correctly. Six. Not too much burden on the conscience of the city, half a dozen. Tell that to the parents who lost their cindered bairns in the city's ash. Tell that to the homeless widows.

6 November

He walks and walks. He needs exhaustion to curb his impotent rage. Let no one think his non-violence comes easy. Today, like many days, he wants to take injustice and hammer rusting nails through its wrist.

7 November–23 December

Inside him, an ocean of darkness. Above, black sky, as if the slow darkness of the prisons he has known will never lift. As if that other sky he sometimes feels is there, that infinite ocean of love, does not have weight enough, substance enough, to fall, to cover him.

24 December

And now they're calling the Great Fire an act of God. God! As if He was the one to pack those bodies under flimsy roofs. As if God had not screamed the loudest.

25 December

He walks and walks and walks. Every day a surrender. Every footstep a prayer.

Imaginary Prisons

after *Carceri d'invenzione* by Giovanni Battista Piranesi, 1745

This is the architecture of remorse. Here you will never stop climbing, one heavy step at a time, your feet no longer yours. See how the levels go up and up. See what an illusion sky has become behind the barred windows. See these broken ladders to the moon. How greedily you reach for rungs that dissolve as you touch them. Already you are dizzy with dreams of escape. The levels go up and up, the steps spiral round and round. It is your first time here. You feel sick. You feel cold. You feel like a child. You want to relieve yourself. This prison will make of you a trapeze artist. You will swing from floor to floor, tight-rope over invisible streets. You will hurl yourself into empty space, that mother of empty space, where the light is strongest, you will fall onto that metal net, then rise again, as from a trampoline. The whole place will turn into a circus, a big top of resurrection and vanishing tricks. You will dream of master keys and unknotting ropes, of learning how to escape straitjackets as you sit under water. But right now, you are unsure if time has ended or has just begun. Is this your future you are leaving behind, or your past you are entering? And how can they be called bridges, these structures that lead nowhere? Welcome to the last days. You have entered the ruins of empire.

After the Door Has Opened

i.m. Hazrat Babajan (d. 1931)

Here, in San Jan Mohammad Street,
dwells she who is no longer she,
whose desire is gone, who waits
for what is already done.

She is *Hafizah* –
one who has learned the Koran by heart.
She has visited the black box at Mecca,
kissed the stone of the Kaaba,
but she chooses the holy slums of Pune,
where hunger shrivels in unshaded heat.

Women break at her feet their coconuts of prayer,
make their supplications for babies.
But she knows the gift of sorrow –
how we may learn to squeeze sugar
out of grief.

She knows walking is always backwards,
the best living a kind of erasure –
each day rubbing out the folly of what went before;
how the greatest millstone of pain
cannot grind the grain of you small enough,
the finest sieve will not make you pure.

Her hair is the white of egrets.
Her face *Gulrukh* – like a rose.
And since the time her life opened
onto the fire that gives God his heat,
she knows the deceit of daylight.

So what if she was Rabia of Basra,
who wrote pleasure in the sand?
She would rather be despised as the thief

who climbed in to steal her final blanket.
Even the best poems should not be worshipped,
but hung out like rags. Words must buckle
at the knees.

Yes, here, in San Jan Mohammad Street,
trades a stall-keeper from whom few want to buy.
Her age – a hundred or more –
small matter as she sits
under the angel of the neem tree –
seven centuries between each feather.

Tea with Simone Weil, Ashford, Kent, 1943

Even in her coat, I can see how thin she is.
She doesn't eat a thing, looks through me
as if somewhere behind me stands the ghost
of myself she would far rather meet,

sits as if she knows the loneliness God carries,
the vast damp weight of it. We could be in church,
our two solitudes candles waiting to be lit.
And I want to ask her why she holds suffering

as the password to God, to explain that equation
she wrote, proving that *malheur*, wretchedness,
is our human equivalent of divine perfection.
I want to ask her what it was like,

being at college with Simone de Beauvoir,
what it was like on the front line in Spain,
in Renault's car factory, but my questions
are as unwanted as the rationed butter and jam.

She sits with no need to justify herself,
not smiling, her wire-rimmed spectacles
keeping me at bay, absorbed in her grief
much as a tree takes in poison,

trying to turn the world back to green.
She's so young, looks so old, I want to say, yes,
of course there's war, but there's also peace,
sleep, food, sex, absinthe. And I start to recite

George Herbert, the poem she too knows
by heart – *Love bade me welcome:*
yet my soul drew back, guilty of dust and sin...
Then she lifts her head, as if once again

hearing the silence at Solesmes Abbey,
those tall walls that can keep out a flood.
I? The unkind, ungrateful? Ah my dear, I cannot
look on thee. Our soft voices drift like moths

towards the steamed-up windows. Perhaps
she'll heed Love's invitation, after all, to *sit*
and eat, but she can't forget what's happening
right now to people speaking her mother-tongue,

pushes away her plate, rises abruptly from her chair.
And before I can stop her, she's stepped out into the rain,
into her final days, her starving body a white stick
tapping its way back to Him through the unremitting dark.

The Artist's View of Surgery

after Barbara Hepworth's hospital drawings 1947–8

Of course she feels at home, when surgeons hold their chisels
the same way she holds hers when hollowing stone.

Fenestration of the Ear might be a self-portrait: hammer
and tiny chisel tapping away at the closed bone of the skull.

That ear – which had been dense and deaf, a solid obstruction –
now a window to let in the wash of Atlantic sea and Cornish rain.

See her standing there for hours, sketching with her pen, enthralled
by those able-to-do-anything hands, moving as a sculptor's might:

so much incising, stitching, such a choreography of arms,
instruments, tense concentration, protracted breath.

Watch her scratch their figures onto gesso with a blade, robe them
like Giotto's saints, bodies poised in stillness, fingers flexed in prayer,

then broaden their shoulders into *quattrocento* giants, men
and women who have stepped out of personality, their faces masked.

Notice how she makes of surgery a ritual, semi-abstract
yet tender, spiralled round that lacuna in the centre –

that invisible place where the eye is drawn – the vanishing point,
the wound – implied, like the unseen hub of a wheel.

And how everything is composed around it, the medics
a Greek chorus, a pantheon of gods at the pivot of creation,

taking the body to a new dimension, the theatre
a liminal realm poised between life and whatever lies beyond.

See her travel to the Venice Biennale, 1950, grow a thick skin
when critics dub her *a dead loss* compared to Henry Moore.

Witness her pleasure as she sits in the Piazza San Marco.
She is not yet divorced. Her elder son has not yet died.

The watery city is celestial. She watches the crowds,
observes they walk differently when they enter the square,

as if the architecture makes them want to stand taller,
the winged lion of St Mark's calling them to look higher.

They are discovering, she later writes, *their innate dignity.*
Read how she *marries* artists and surgeons, their shared

haptic skill, their coaxing of light and space into what is
opaque, cumbersome. Note how you covet such

high purpose, even though you know it can take over a life,
lose the human being to abstraction, risk ending in flames.

Barbara Hepworth Considers the Visitors at Trewyn

They love to ask about the fire:
those scorch marks on my living room floor.

Or they sit in the garden hoping
an angel might appear

looking like me – red gingham scarf,
a chisel behind each ear.

The holes are where we meet –
for them, a weightless place of possibilities,

for me, the hollow of what's missed –
the inside edge of stone, unpolished bronze,

sounds like the mirage of sea inside
a shell – an ocean of far-off moments.

And I want to tell them it's as true now:
there is no fixed point

of light – everything still asks
to be touched, walked through.

A Piece of Cloth

for Nasrin Sotoudeh

Where will the lashes fall? On the shoulders, or the ribs?
Who will lift her when she sinks to the floor? What lakes
will catch her blood? Has she been too proud of her back,
the way she rode a bike or stayed atop a horse? Has she
been too proud of her husband, children, lawyer's
credentials? But the Prophet, peace be upon him, surely
knows there are different kinds of pride, false and true,
different kinds of men, false and true. Is not the *hijab*
a piece of cloth like any other, pegged on washing lines
along with shirts, sheets, pants? Who bid a man wedge
the Quran beneath his armpit to flay this woman's back
until the blood is a river and the bones laid bare? Surely
the Prophet, peace be upon him, calls upon the angel
Jibril to intervene. Surely the Prophet's thirteen wives,
mothers of the believers, sing in praise of these beautiful
girls who drape their *hijabs* on branches of the pomegranate
trees. Surely they liken the cloths that flutter round
the fruits to uncaged birds trying their wings.

The Woman Who Lives at the Back of the Quaker Meeting House

crops her hair like spikes on a scrubbing brush
stands on her head so she can know the rush

of emptiness, hangs prayer flags in the rain
like sanguine laundry, knows that a plus sign

is made up of two minuses, does not
berate her body, does not separate

the world into giraffes and foxes, lets
her fridge-top serve as a Buddhist shrine, sits

in her doorway to sew a quilt as white
and green as fields of daisies, does not eat

much, does not fear the company of the dead,
spends her days uprooting weeds in the graveyard,

clearing grass from half-moons of graves that gleam
like rising planets, has no desire to seem

younger than she is, does not own a car,
does have a smile I would sell my house for.

In This Period of Strange Calm

I have become a distant witness
to other people's suffering,
the way a woman in ancient Greece,
say, whose hours are spent worrying
if yesterday's dish of food will stretch
to another meal, or how many goats
are lost on Mount Pelion, is dumbfounded
to hear what is happening skies away
in Delphi, it being hard for one
with simple ideas about goodness
to understand the necessity of sacrifice
to appease gods who have, apparently,
reached their limit of enduring human folly.
Perhaps she too stands outside
under a full pink moon, sends thanks
to white-robed figures attending
the dead, tears off leaves of oregano,
sage, wild mint, raises her hands
in prayer towards the gods hiding
on Mount Olympus, says –
This is enough, now, surely this sacrifice
is enough, we can change our ways –
then waits under the chestnut trees
for signs she has been heard.

Lockdown as a Kind of Pilgrimage

One day I will relive this as a time of elegy,
of quiet reckoning, try to recall the moat
of silence that circles the house, how chairs
and sofas have turned into islands,
the floor an ocean. My sacred journeys
in the world were noisier affairs,
no peace at all, the manic pace of India,
frantic rickshaw rides, poverty thrusting itself
into my face along with traffic, frangipani.
Now I'm watching through skylights as if this
is my meditation, the way clouds slowly drift,
collect, disperse, the way even the blue backdrop
is an illusion. Somewhere, presumably,
something is watching us with equal amazement,
equal awe, as we drift, collect, disperse.
How can a time of suffering feel so holy?
Surely we're being asked to go inwards,
go deeper, beyond shale and sandstone,
below hidden blocks and habit patterns
of our lives to the deepest source. Why else
are the usual sites of blessing closed –
Lourdes, Mecca, Jerusalem's holy sepulchre –
unless to remind us we must find love here,
in our cells of seclusion, or not find it anywhere.

III. Among Mortals

At Foggintor Quarry

I'm a discus throw from the prison,
sitting by the quarry pool, weighing up
my own deeds, good and bad. I keep
so still the birds don't notice me.
Wagtails, the chirpy whiteness of their
backsides insouciant in the wind.
And here's a runner, black dog at his heels,
sneaking through crannies in the stones.
Below his shorts, the man's legs, strong
and brown, remind me of my ex-husband.
He too came to Dartmoor, to live
and die. But we missed each other, mostly,
even in our meeting, like wood floating
at different speeds. Sometimes I think
I've missed everyone I've met.
It's what the word *dis-appointment* means.
Did I ever properly talk with Graham,
who's dying? What can you give someone
who has to leave everything behind?
Would he want a share of my faith
in the afterlife, carrying him over on sheets
of fine Egyptian cotton, the tall figure
of Anubis at the side of the bed,
that canine head knowing where they're going,
a silver ankh in his hand like a key?

A Medic Learns to Darn in the Dissecting Room

I'd told myself I'd pack my heart in ice. And when
I learned to sew, it would be mattress stitch
or purse-string sutures, swaged needles, polypropylene.

But here I am threading a needle's eye with wool
the colour of barley, listening to the artist
as she teaches us to weave over and under, weft and warp,

our stitches neat as lines on graph paper, their repeated
refrains a kind of prayer, sanguine, lifting
the weight of so much mortality stacked against us.

We are to let our minds wander as we darn
and I patiently fill the hole of an Arran blue sweater,
become the man who thrust his arm into

this threadbare sleeve, propped his elbows on a bench
while he dismantled carburettors, snagged the cuffs
when he and his young son picked blackberries.

When we return to the bodies, lent to us
for a year, they too are full of story,
every inch shaped by its missing life –

this badly-set wrist fractured in a street fight;
that scarred and stretch-marked abdomen
that has brought forth child after child; months

of fierce passion chronicled in swallows swooping
down a shoulder blade. And I fall in love with it all
in a new way, this riddle of life inside death,

stand now in front of each derelict self
with tender curiosity – with the precision
of someone darning, who knows all our bodies

are on loan, full of holes, held together by thread
after invisible thread, the touch intimate,
the hand at work remarkably steady.

Where Bluebells Are Thickest

I lie down, look past worms of catkins
to a sky buoyant enough to persuade me
I'm floating on a salty sea and can never drown.

Thin drifts of cloud remind me of friends I've lost
this winter, the way each year bowls out another couple,
wickets toppling after too few sixes.

When I walk to the road again, my head's leaking
birdsong. Cars are stalled behind a huge white horse,
summoned from the sun for some heavenly chariot.

The flanks are brushed to a gleam, the mane combed
as if every hair of its head were numbered.
The girl steering it has tiny wrists and fat-free thighs,

and she bobs like a cork, barely a teenager. If only,
I think, the soul could ride the body like this.
If only I were half mortal, half horse

of the apocalypse, able to stop men in their tracks
as she does, stop the whole world in its foolish tracks,
ride into an afternoon torn wide open.

The Chinvat Bridge

I think of it more and more, this bridge, whether it will
shrink or sway under the weight of my sins. It's known
to shapeshift – for some as wide as a motorway, others
the gamble of a hair's breadth. Some say the bridge
is arched, the way a back can arch in delight, others,
that it tapers until it will take nothing but the feet
of the entirely dispossessed. Often I wish for rope,
a bridge of hemp so taut and fine I might crawl
in stealthy silence over that unfathomable drop.
But mostly I long for wood, simple planks planed
from apple or beech. Then I'll find courage in the smell,
recall those walks when only goodness seemed possible,
borrow light from long afternoons we lay on the lawn
surrounded by larkspur and cranesbill. There was no fear
then. God seemed to show himself in the clouds.
Tonight, though, the bridge is packed like Waterloo
at rush hour, everyone pushing on to somewhere
unseen. They say there's a House of Song on the far side,
bands playing your favourite music to lure you over.
But tonight I can hear nothing but barking – black dogs
with two heads and four eyes who guard the parapet.
They howl like that when some soul lost on the bridge –
mother, husband, child, friend – tries to find their way
back. I know that sound well. Music won't drown it.

The Hunger of Colour

As a brush is sometimes
unable to pause

even when the canvas
is finished

and paint spills beyond the frame
in sheer exuberance

so I want my life
to eat my death

like *Harmony in Red*
by Matisse

the way he foils the commission
for a study in blue

spreads crimson over
plate and pomegranate

the way the patterned tablecloth
becomes the wallpaper

In a Worldly Setting

When I sense your presence those first days
out of your body, I want you to be an oracle,
to tell me what it's like in the hinterland.
Do you stand in the ruins of a stained stairwell?
Do you feel you've lost your keys but still belong
in the building? I want you to uncork the mystery,
to share that hybrid state, half-shoulder, half-wing,
as you dip into the wisdom between lives,
perhaps become party to the first word man ever
uttered and what will be the last. Is it true we find
what we expect in death? Those final months,
while you readied yourself to return to smoke,
were you preparing to meet your wife and
unborn child, stolen from you while you slept?
I've often wondered if that grief – unparaded,
like all your feelings – was what slowly stole
your breathing too. But now you're buoyant,
resilient, your soul commanding, tangible,
full of your old lift, your silence telling me
this is better than you'd expected, better than
anything you'd taken death, or 'God', to be,
and Whitman was right: *Death is different and far*
luckier than you suppose. Even when you leave,
snatched away before you can share too much,
the room holds its joyful intensity, as if you'd
happily bequeath more. Then I re-read your poems
for their prescience, half-hidden clues that rise
like almost visible spires of a city that has slid
into the sea. I remember the night you travelled
cross country for the launch of my book.
No orchids, no jay feathers, just this presence
of you – full of heft, lumbering downstairs
to the stage – a kind of embarrassed love.

In Which I Ask Forgiveness of My Body

Dear body, I am trying so hard to love you,
even as you lose your beauty. I give thanks
for the miracles, the way you fetch and carry,

retrieve clean air, piss out yellow poison daily.
I proclaim the wonder of your ligaments
and nerves, dozens of bones in the foot,

trillions of synapses firing in the brain,
the kindness of this tireless drumming heart.
Yet still, I dream of sloughing you off

so I can return sleek, unlined, surf
the inside of waves, fall in love again
for the first time, make heads turn.

For you, dear body, are all remnant. You are
tired flesh that can never be ironed smooth.
Forgive me, old snail, my lack of tenderness.

You've borne my soul so patiently
upon your crumbling back all these years,
bear it still as we crawl towards our black hole.

Oh body, there is no health in me. Teach me
your uncomplaining love, your path of selfless
service, even as you fail.

Clothed in Mud and Feathers

In dreams you can let yourself feel the fear
you've denied all day, admit the virus dogs you
as you go back to the college where you taught,
break into a sweat as you try to get library books
back onto shelves before their wisdom runs out of date.
Panic rises as other staff loiter, fail to observe
the necessary metre or more, and you want
to shove a tombstone in their face, resurrect
O-level Latin with some apt *memento mori* –
Omnia mors perimit et nulli miseretur.
What do these women think they're doing,
finishing their admin, eating cheese sandwiches
for lunch? Why, for that matter, are you here,
putting your history of ideas to bed instead
of self-isolating? Perhaps your dream knows
something you don't, perhaps it's time at last
to write that letter as appendage to your will,
say exactly where you wish your books/art/
ear-rings/body to go. Let's face it, you've had
many epiphanies, many opportunities to reflect
on ultimate things, yet still you carry on
as if you're more than a bag of bones, as if
when you wake to the sound of neighbours
mowing the lawn, the April sun calling you down,
it matters to attend to your own garden.
You think death makes any distinction
between tasks done and undone? You can
never be ready. Trust your dream.
Death destroys all and pities no-one.

Rowing

Here you are, near the edge of the world, rowing
across a vast lake. You thought you knew the water,
but now the sun sets earlier, the distance seems blacker

and your courage has shrunk. You are tired of having
to re-invent yourself. Some things, you think, you should
be able to take for granted: that place you imagine

most people start from, the block of love they push
against to start sprinting. It astonishes you so much
of your life has worked – marriage, family, friends –

as if they found something in you that you didn't.
You rest the oars of your boat. You are weary of acting
out of fear. If the bird of night comes, let it come.

The air is still. In woods at the edge of the lake,
owls call. To your surprise, you like it here,
the water beneath you the depth of several trees.

How long is it since you did this, sat in a boat
and studied the textures of darkness?
You feel you have rowed into the centre of a tear.

You remember the Sufi saying that God sees
a black ant on a black stone in the darkest night.
The sky closes over you like an eyelid.

Harvest

My friend Linda, a poet, died unexpectedly this week.
She was ten years younger than me. I keep seeing her

that afternoon at one of my classes, when a mallard
had wandered onto my back lawn, God knows why.

Linda was the one who knew how to approach it, talk to it, coax it
into a box and take it home to her pond. She was practical like that.

The shock of mortality changes things, makes them clearer,
scissors black silhouettes against sunlight like a daguerreotype.

For years, I wanted to be like a man, to put my feet
under their privileged table. Now I'm happy to not belong,

to spend my time wresting mercy from its opposite,
beauty from mud and grit. I don't care anymore

who wears the medals or feathers. I'm just thankful
to have arrived at the harvest of myself, to have come through,

able to look back on all the wounding as someone
trying to stab water. And when I think of Linda,

I can't help catching some exuberance,
as if death is the same kind of excitement

that comes each morning when darkness lifts.
That simple happiness.

Among Mortals

On the train down, I listened to *The Song
of Achilles*, thought how hard it is to unlearn
a sense of destiny. You always expected gold,

I was a lesser mortal hired in to hone
your words, blunt some, whet others to hit
their distant mark. We had many battles

over the years, long periods of silence.
Only when the oracle foresaw your death –
deferred many times, never cancelled –

did we manage a lasting truce.
And now the other mourners have left
I stay behind, watch October sun cling

to your hollow in the ground. You seem
to strike there like a tree rooting,
like Achilles planting his feet to target

his shimmering spear. And when arrows
hit me in the chest – longing, fire, ferocious
gratitude – I know it's you, asking for more,

like those gods who are sick to death
of perfection and want only to slide into bed
with the body of a mortal.

How to Love the Dead

When I turn to poets for help, Jack Gilbert,
who knew all about beds and bodies, human
love and its unmaking, offers me titles like
'Cherishing What Isn't' or 'How to Love the Dead'.
He encourages my use of unfashionable language:
heft, tenderly, meanwhile, marred, tells me the nine years
since his passing have stretched into the no-time
of legend, less exile than living in a land you know
you don't quite deserve, like his sojourn in Greece,
that perpetual wonder of islands sleeping in the sea,
sand almost too hot to walk on with bare feet.
And yes, I hear him say, it's fine to improvise,
to imitate his best lines – *the ruthless furnace
of this world, Mortality like a cello inside him.*

#Better than Angels

That murmuration of starlings I saw at new year
on the Somerset levels: four million of them,

giant ink blots in the sky melding into dark formations
above water and peat. I posted photos on Facebook:

#better than angels. The universe, thank God, is more
intelligent than we are. The soul in everything: *anima mundi.*

If it takes another flood to bring us to our senses, it will happen.
Everything is connected. Even as being in a body gets harder,

we have to let our selves be worn away, dissolve, till we are
more river than rock, able to move with the current, tide,

pull of the moon, to become as transparent as spirit,
compassion sitting inside us like water. Love without

hair splitting. Love that puts itself in the balance, light
as a feather, yet muscled enough to carry the world.

When My Body is Pulled from Me

there'll be no time to apologise
to my lover as angels push him to one side,
no chance to say farewell to my breasts,
tenderness, toe nails, all of which have served me
for decades without complaint. I'll just be
swimming in the pool of the day, unshriven,
unshaven, when I'm yanked out by the roots,
my mind asking *what the fuck is happening?*
my soul lifted into the astonishment of a blue
and yellow moment, sifted into the shape
of something weaker yet stronger than
I've ever known – breeze, wind, monsoon,
mistral, boreas, sirocco, white squall, zephyr –
every kind of hurricane and whisper.

The Golden Bough

handed to guardians of the underworld was mistletoe,
garlands plucked for luck to keep shadows at bay.
Soldiers in the First World War had sprigs sewn onto cards,
hopeful amulets. *Mystyldene. Devil's fuge. All-heal.*

But the legend I like most is of Frigga, Norse goddess
of love, queen of *seidr* – magic – who could summon events
into being, robe herself with falcon plumes, turn into a bird.
Yet when her son, Balder, was killed by an arrow

crafted from mistletoe, she could not save him, but wept
and wept – what mother would not grieve her lost child?
– wept over the fatal twig until her tears formed into pearls,
lucent emblems of her unstoppable love.

I think of her when I walk in parkland in winter, where poplars
foster baubles of mistletoe, perfect spheres cradled against
an impassive sky. I think of my own son, many losses,
and the different endings of Frigga's story: how some say

Balder was never restored to life and the world was plunged
into darkness; others, that the gods repented when they saw
his mother's sorrow, and she stood in a delirium of gratitude
under the mistletoe, happy to kiss anyone who passed.

I stand here now in the bleak light as she must have done then,
back pressed against bark – apple, hawthorn, lime – looking up
at the stark lattice of branches, their bunches of mistletoe harboured
like refugee moons. And I want to cry out, as Frigga did,

to the air and birds and new-found tenderness of the world
that love is surely bigger than grief, than death.
Come, stand with me beneath these white berries of love.
Let me hold you, kiss you.

Life Shocks

I'm looking for words to catch strands of fresh willow,
the first skylark pulling me up towards forgotten
height and blue,

when the order of service honouring your life
slips from the shelf and there you are –
your eyes, your large ears – *all the better to hear you with* –

that outrageous smile they failed to bury.
You always said life delivers its shocks in two ways:
limiting, to remind us we are not gods, *evoking*,

to help us know the love that summons all this
into being. So now, this first spring without you,
the earth struck by war again,

I'm learning to bear the beauty of stitchwort,
kindness, birdsong, all these resurrections
of our lives, their sweet insurgencies.

Notes

The title 'Love Leans over the Table' is adapted from the lines of the epigraph (my translation), which are verse 9 of the 14th-century love lyric 'Blow Northerne Wind', MS Harley 2253 in the British Library. I found this poem through the website of Anna Tam, who set the lyrics to music. http://www.annatam.co.uk

Part I

'Hildegard's Remedy'
Hildegard von Bingen, 1098–1179, was a German Benedictine abbess, composer, writer, mystic, who coined the word 'viriditas', or 'greening', as a theological term to convey the healing and creative power of nature. She left recipes for healing remedies in her *Book of Simple Medicine* 1161.

'Letter to Nietzsche'
Friedrich Nietzsche, 1844–1900, exerted a strong influence on modern thought with his secular thought, contempt for religion and famous declaration that 'God is dead.' In 1889, aged 45, he suffered a physical and mental collapse leading to complete loss of his intellectual faculties.

'The Day Meher Baba Died'
Meher Baba, born Pune, India, 1894, died Meherazad, 25 February 1969, 12.15pm. A copy of Leslie Hutchinson singing Cole Porter's 'Begin the Beguine' was played at the interment, and Baba's tomb shrine at Meherabad, in the state of Maharashtra, has become a site of pilgrimage.

'The Night I Grew Old'
The Lady of Shalott was painted by Pre-Raphaelite John William Waterhouse, 1894.

'Don't Think These Doors Will Ever Close'
Dorothea Tanning, 1910–2012, was an American Surrealist artist married to Max Ernst.

'After Reading Wendy Pratt's *When I Think of My Body as a Horse*'
Wendy Pratt's collection of this title was published by Smith Doorstop in 2021.

'Coming to Terms With'
These lines are an improvisation on words from trauma theorist Cathy Caruth: 'Trauma is a break in the mind's experience of time'.

'My Father Tries to Make Amends'
The lines *'hearken O daughter, I am poured out like water, my heart is like wax'* are adapted from Psalm 22:14: 'I am poured out like water, And all My bones are out of joint; My heart is like wax; It has melted within Me.'

'Revisiting *The Garden of Earthly Delights* at the Prado'
My first book, *Fantasy: The Literature of Subversion* (Methuen, 1981), featured part of Hieronymus Bosch's painting on its cover.

'Blue'
The album *Blue* by Joni Mitchell came out in June 1971. The phrases quoted are from the track 'All I Want.'

'Stroke'
Gay Clifford, 1943–1998, was the author of *The Transformations of Allegory* (Routledge, 1974). A medieval scholar, she taught at the University of Warwick, then at University College, London. On Christmas Eve 1984, she suffered a major cerebral haemorrhage, which left her memory and intellect impaired.

Part II

'Tilting'
This triolet is inspired by Marie Howe's 'Annunciation' from *The Kingdom of Ordinary Time* (Norton, 2008).

'St Bede: From Winter to Winter'
The Venerable Bede lived from 672 to 755. His famous parable in *The Ecclesiastical History of the English People* (731) likens life to a sparrow's flight through a warm hall. I borrowed the opening from a poem I am now unable to trace and would be grateful to be able to acknowledge the source.

'Rabia and the Thief'

Rabia of Basra, *c.* 717–801, a Sufi mystic and poet, was the first woman to become a Muslim saint.

'When I Wonder What It Was Like to Be an Anchorite'

Between 1100 and 1539, 780 anchorites in England, mostly women, were enclosed in tiny structures attached to the side of a church. They chose their imprisonment, from which they would never be released. The act of committing anchorites to their cells was accompanied by funeral rites, to signify their death to the world. I am indebted to E. A. Jones, *Hermits and Anchorites in England 1200–1550* (Manchester University Press, 2019) and to Henrietta Leyser, *Medieval Women: A Social History of Women in England* 450–1500 (Weidenfeld & Nicholson, 1995) for my research.

'One Little Roome, an Every Where'

The title is borrowed from John Donne's poem 'The Good-Morrow', 1633. 'And now good-morrow to our waking souls / Which watch not one another out of fear; / For love, all love of other sights controls, / And makes one little roome an everywhere.' The phrases *'washed with milk and fitly set, head is filled with dew'* are from the Song of Solomon 5:12.

'The Recluse Tells of Her Love'

The vocabulary here is taken from Richard Rolle's 14th-century text *The Fire of Love.*

'Ancrene Wisse'

Initially written in 1200 by a man for his three sisters as they were enclosed for life in cells 12 feet square, *The Ancrene Wisse* became a manual for female anchorites.

'A Kind of Divorce'

Records show that, on one occasion, a married couple were enclosed for life as anchorites.

'The Long Text'

After a vision during severe illness, Julian of Norwich, *c.* 1343–1416, wrote *Revelations of Divine Love.* An early version was extended over years into a more elaborate work known as the *Long Text.*

'The Boisterous Sobbings of Margery Kempe'

The title of this poem is borrowed from Elizabeth Smart's poem 'Margery Kempe' in *A Bonus* (1977). Margery Kempe, *c.*1373–1438, was the mother of fourteen children, part of a family of wealthy merchants in King's Lynn, Norfolk. She dictated her auto-biography to a priest, claimed to have visitations from Christ, made pilgrimages to Europe, and was infamous for her endless and dramatic weeping in public places. Julian of Norwich defended her visions as authentic.

'An Anchorite Laments the Destruction of Her Cell in Henry VIII's Dissolution of the Monasteries, 1537'

When Henry VIII disbanded monasteries, convents and other religious property, anchorite cells were destroyed and the women forced back into the community; unless they had families to take them in, they became vagrants.

'John Donne Dreams His Still-Born Son Lives'

John Donne's wife Anne died on 15 August 1617, five days after giving birth to their twelfth child, a still-born baby.

'Batter My Heart'

Meher Baba, 1894–1969, said John Donne was his favourite Western poet, and Donne's Holy Sonnet XIV 'Batter my heart, three-person'd God' his favourite of Donne's poems, which he memorised while a student at Deccan College, Pune.

'John Donne Arriving in Heaven'

The title of this poem is taken from a painting by Stanley Spencer (1910). Some of the phrases are from Donne, some of the ideas come from the teachings of Meher Baba.

'George Fox Learns of the Great Fire'

George Fox, 1624–1691, a Dissenter who founded the Quakers, was repeatedly imprisoned for his unconventional beliefs. He was released from Scarborough Prison on 1 September 1666; the Great Fire of London began on 2 September, raged for three days and persisted for weeks. It destroyed the homes of 70,000 out of London's 80,000 inhabitants. The death toll most likely ran into thousands, though the official number of deaths was just six.

'Imaginary Prisons'

Giovanni Battista Piranesi, 1720–1778, was an architect and artist who between 1745 and 1750 produced etchings of Rome and of fictitious prisons, vaults with endless stairs and machines.

'After the Door Has Opened'

The shrine of Hazrat Babajan, a Muslim 'Perfect Master', is in the Char Bawdi district of Pune, India. Until her death in 1931, Babajan spent her last 24 years living here under a neem tree and, in 1913, revealed to Meher Baba his spiritual identity. She was said to be the reincarnation of Rabia of Basra. Her family name was Gulrukh (rose-faced).

'Tea with Simone Weil, Ashford, Kent, 1943'

French mystic, philosopher and political activist Simone Weil, 1909–1943, developed a mathematical model to defend the value of 'affliction' as a way of attaining God. Albert Camus called her 'the only great spirit of our time.' She spent some time in seclusion at the Abbey at Solesmes and memorised George Herbert's sonnet 'Love'. She died in Ashford, Kent.

'The Artist's View of Surgery'

Sculptor Barbara Hepworth, 1903–1975, made over 70 drawings while observing surgeons at work, notably Norman Capener in Exeter, and ear, nose and throat specialist Edward Garnett Passe. The drawings, from 1947 to 1950, celebrate the recent creation of the National Health Service, presenting medical staff as semi-divine Giotto-like figures. In the late 1950s she gave a lecture which drew parallels between the work of sculptors and surgeons. Her eldest child Paul was killed in a plane crash in 1953 while serving with the Royal Air Force.

'Barbara Hepworth Considers the Visitors at Trewyn'

Hepworth died in a fire from one of her unextinguished cigarettes at her studio at Trewyn, St Ives. The final lines are hers.

'A Piece of Cloth'

In March 2019, Nasrin Sotoudeh, a human rights lawyer in Tehran, was sentenced to 38 years in prison and 148 lashes for defending Iranian women's right to remove their hijab in public. Under Islamic law, the man doing the flogging should hold under his arm a copy of the Quran.

'Lockdown as a Kind of Pilgrimage'

During the 2020 Covid pandemic, most sites of spiritual pilgrimage were closed.

Part III

'A Medic Learns to Darn in the Dissecting Room'

In 2014, medics training at King's College Anatomy School, London, worked with resident artist Celia Pym, who encouraged them to connect with human stories as they darned clothes.

'The Chinvat Bridge'

In Zoroastrianism, the Chinvat bridge is the bridge of judgement separating life from death, where souls are sifted. Two four-eyed dogs guard the bridge, which changes in appearance depending on the righteousness of the soul.

'How to Love the Dead'

'How to Love the Dead' and 'Cherishing what Isn't' are titles of poems by American poet Jack Gilbert, 1925–2012. The final quotes are his.

'Among Mortals'

The Song of Achilles is a novel by Madeline Miller, published in 2011.

'The Golden Bough'

In Roman mythology, the golden bough was a branch of mistletoe, sacred to Prosperine (Persephone in Greek mythology), who spends half the year in the underworld. In Book VI of Virgil's Aeneid, the golden bough enables Aeneas to travel safely through the underworld. James Frazer's study *The Golden Bough* (1890) draws parallels between many world religions where death and rebirth/resurrection are central metaphors.

'Life Shocks'

'Life Shocks' borrows its title from the late Sophie Sabbage's study *Life Shocks* (Hodder and Stoughton, 2018) which followed her bestselling book *The Cancer Whisperer* (Hodder and Stoughton, 2016) and uses ideas from the late Dr K Bradford Brown who set up the More to Life training.

Two Rivers Press has been publishing in and about Reading
since 1994. Founded by the artist Peter Hay (1951–2003),
the press continues to delight readers, local and further afield,
with its varied list of individually designed,
thought-provoking books.